Poetic Praises

Patti A. Tucker

TRILOGY CHRISTIAN PUBLISHERS
TUSTIN, CA

Trilogy Christian Publishers
A Wholly Owned Subsidiary of Trinity Broadcasting Network
2442 Michelle Drive
Tustin, CA 92780

For information, address Trilogy Christian Publishing

Rights Department, 2442 Michelle Drive, Tustin, Ca 92780.

For information about special discounts for bulk purchases, please contact Trilogy Christian Publishing.

Manufactured in the United States of America

10 9 8 7 6 5 4 3 2 1

Library of Congress Cataloging-in-Publication Data is available.

ISBN 978-1-63769-440-4

ISBN 978-1-63769-441-1 (ebook)

Dedication

I would like to dedicate *Poetic Praises* to all the spiritual leaders that have touched my life. Billy Graham was the first messenger that impacted my life as I watched many of his crusades on TV and came to know Christ.

Later, the teachings of Joyce Meyer and Dr. Charles Stanley served as pivotal examples and directed me with a deeper understanding of God.

To all those who have led me and helped in my journey, thank you.

I would like to thank the team at Trilogy Christian Publishing for bringing *Poetic Praises* to life.

Contents

Foreword

Patti Tucker's writings celebrate the strength of a military wife of fifty-one years. After retirement, she continues serving humanity in the community.

> Instead, we were like young children among you. Just as a nursing mother cares for her children, so we cared for you. Because we loved you so much, we were delighted to share with you not only the gospel of God but our lives as well.
>
> 1 Thessalonians 2:7-8 (NIV)

"Early in her life, as her husband was serving his country, Patti was serving using her spiritual gifts for her family and for soldiers' families in a variety of ways for Jesus. Patti developed her ministry, 'Touchpoints Ministry,' to care for the elderly and the homebound shut-ins in the community.

"The verse above and Patti's writings paint a beautiful picture of a mentor and parent. Sharing God's good news is important, but so is sharing life. As of this writing, I am privileged to have read much about Patti's passion for life but also passion for others. Her writings invite others into her life, they get to observe the passion that she truly cares for and loves people. Patti's Poetic Praises will supplement and be added to my current daily devotional readings."

—Howard Williams, Corporate Executive,
Dir. Emeritus Abound Credit Union

"I speak with authority when I say Patti Tucker lives the life she talks about. The hope, patriotism, faith, and love of God she expresses in these pages are fruits of her spirit. These poems are spiritual. Patti writes from the spiritual depths of her walk with God. In these times of pandemic as so many are experiencing profound pain, allow me to prescribe this: number one—always pray; number two—read Patti's poems."

—Rev. Carl S. Young Jr.
Associate Pastor for Congregational Care,
Ebenezer Baptist Church, Atlanta, Georgia

"Patti highlights the timelessness of scripture as she beautifully navigates the gap between the Word and the world by applying it to specific trials and emotions we face today...Her poetry gives a sense of comfort, yet at the same time, it challenges one to action."

—Colonel (Retired) Brian Sperling

"Poetic Praises is the result of Patti Tucker's sincere and committed faith in our Lord and Savior Jesus Christ. These poems are a revelation of God's love, grace, and mercy towards His children. Patti's use of poetic prose will transcend you in the presence of God Almighty, and the rhythmic standards are a voice that allows God to speak to the soul and spirit with assurance of hope, joy, and peace."

—Lieutenant Colonel (Retired) Mackberth Williams
PhD Candidate, Values Driven Ministries

"Poetic Praises will definitely assist in the mental and spiritual part of a healthy life balance."

—Command Sergeant Major (Ret.) William (Joe) Gainey
1st Senior Enlister Advisor to the Chairman,
Joint Chiefs of Staff

"Enjoy the passion Patti has in her heart for the Lord and her excellence of expression. God bless her."

—John Poland, CEO, Christian Values Coalition

"If you have read Patti's first book, Salute, you will see how very dedicated she is to her faith, family, and friends. I am inspired by her second book, and I know you will be as well. God bless you, Patti!"

—Judy LaPorte, a forever friend

"'Terrible Tuesday' is wonderfully expressive... displays a unique perspective and original creativity... Editor's Choice Award Winner!"

—Managing Editor, poetry.com and International Library of Poetry

Poetic Praises: Time

How are you spending your time?
Hopefully using it wisely and honoring God with respect ever sublime.
We are each given the same amount,
So it is important to be productive and make it count.

There are so many ways we can do outreach,
But we must be obedient to seek and teach.
We don't want to waste this precious gift,
As we have been granted just so much to encourage and lift.

How are you spending your time?
Hopefully using it wisely and honoring God with respect ever sublime.
It is uncertain how much time we possess,
So now is when we should stand and help all under duress.

Be very careful, then, how you live—not as unwise but as wise, making the most of every opportunity, because the days are evil. Therefore do not be foolish, but understand what the Lord's will is.

Ephesians 5:15-17 (NIV)

Section 1:

God and His Attributes

"The Lord is righteous in all his ways and kind in all his works" (Psalm 145:17, ESV).

Son of God

A supernatural and perfect man who walked the earth,
Came to redeem us all and was manifested by a virgin birth.
This man, who alone never committed a sin,
Was ever so humble, tempted, and tried by many men.

He alone showed us all the way,
The righteous path we must travel and stay.
A magnificent aura that could only please and call us,
Although addressed by many Holy names, He was called Jesus.

He bore each one of our sins on a cross through crucifixion,
We can have eternal life when we accept Him and experience resurrection.
Now is the time to accept the Son of God and be given freedom,
To be assured of our heavenly home in His kingdom.

Faith

The substance of what is hoped for,
What is not seen but allows us to trust and worry no more.

Putting all our doubts and fears aside,
God will intervene, and we can rest and abide.

Believing with all our heart and mind,
We will accomplish supernatural feats and find.

Even as small as a mustard seed,
Faith can move mountains and intercede.

To grow in faith is a continuing process,
But one worth pursuing regardless of doubt or duress.

Gift of Grace

What is this gift of grace?
The ultimate pardon Jesus bestows to allow sin to be erased.
No works or money can buy this gift for us,
Only by the supernatural power that Jesus does.

To be cleansed and redeemed by this act
Is a joy indescribable and a biblical fact.
It is the undeniable love only God can provide,
The work it accomplishes brings peace and results we can't hide.

What is this gift of grace?
The ultimate pardon Jesus bestows to allow sin to be erased.
In the natural, it is an act undeserved,
But because of the perfect will of God, He will preserve.

Our Refuge

In our refuge, I find complete rest and peace,
A place of safety, calmness, and where worries cease.
Do you know this perfect place of protection?
Where we can be assured of tranquility and avoid all condemnation.

Only believers have this promised shelter and hiding place,
A serene sanctuary that is granted free due to His amazing grace.
Heartache, sorrow, and burdens our Heavenly Father will ultimately bear,
In the refuge, where we find an abundance of care.

Do you know this perfect place of protection?
Where we can be assured of tranquility and avoid all condemnation.
Whatever storm you are going through, our refuge is a place of defense,
Where you will find our Mighty God will offer complete recompense.

A Lifeline

Are you in need of a lifeline?
Someone you can call on through every tough time.
In these days we are now living,
We find hatred, violence, and not enough giving.

What has happened to our fellow man?
Looking out for selfish interests and walking away from his own clan.
An evil spirit that seems to be on the rise,
Causing division, destruction, and calamity right before our eyes.

Where do we go to find that one salvation?
A place that will deliver us from every wrong deed and temptation.
There is only one lifeline that can rescue from any trial or storm,
The one perfect stronghold called Jesus to completely transform.

The Ultimate Physician

The ultimate physician can heal and restore any affliction,
His power can remove every disease and deliver from all addiction.
No sickness, heartache, or amount of pain,
Can ever triumph when His divine intervention destroys every bondage and chain.

When we trust and truly believe,
There are no boundaries or limits to the miracles we can receive.
Not only can He heal every human soul,
But can mend a broken world and make it whole.

The ultimate physician can heal and restore any affliction,
His power can remove every disease and deliver from all addiction.
We must turn to the ultimate physician and repent
To restore our world of evil and disconnect.

One Name

There is only one name that has absolute power and can save,
The one who unconditionally sacrificed and gave.
Whatever trial we face or burdens we bear,
There is just one name we can rely and call on in prayer.

One name can calm every fear,
Bind up our wounds, and wipe away every tear.
One name that will provide refuge and protection,
And guide us on the path of sound direction.

There is only one name that has absolute power and can save,
The one who unconditionally sacrificed and gave.
The one name that I will forever praise
Is my Redeemer, Jesus, I will proclaim all my days.

Only One Hope

In a world of darkness, only one hope is our source,
And that one hope is supplied by the one that won't let us lose course.
Putting our trust in anything earthly we think may satisfy,
Will only bring disillusionment and heartache that won't gratify.

Whenever we are on a broken path and all seems lost,
We can be assured our salvation is secured by the cross.
Struggles with doubt, fear, and anxiety
Can be confidently calmed in times of trial and adversity.

Putting our trust in anything earthly we think may satisfy,
Will only bring disillusionment and heartache that won't gratify.
Only one hope has the power to rescue and save,
And that hope is Jesus who overcame and conquered the grave.

The Greatest Friend

The greatest friend we will ever find
Is the one who is rich in mercy, loyal, and kind.
Where we can find compassion and hope in times of darkness,
Someone that will hold our hand and fill our souls with calmness.

A friend that will walk with us through each step of uncertainty,
The one that will comfort each heartache and reign forever with us in eternity.
Just as a seed that must be watered to grow,
This genuine friendship must be cultivated and nourished to maintain a steady flow.

When we are lost, lonely, and overwhelmed by rejection,
He will light our path, provide hope, and give us sound direction.
The greatest friend is the one we can call on through prayer,
One that will provide wisdom and willingly take our burdens to bear.

The greatest friend we will ever find
Is the one who is rich in mercy, loyal, and kind.
How can we find and keep such a loyal friend?
By seeking the Bible, receiving His invitation to salvation,
And forever maintaining peace within.

The Greatest Love

The greatest love the world will ever know
Is the one our Heavenly Father bestows.
A love so unselfish and pure,
Anyone can receive if willing to surrender and rest assured.

A love unfailing, patient, and kind,
Only in the arms of God can we find;
An act which is filled with pure devotion,
A propitiatory choice made not just on emotion.

A forgiving spirit that holds no bitterness,
The true giving heart that flows with genuine tenderness.
The greatest love that was ever given
Was the oblation on their cross to allow us to be forgiven.

When God Winks

Have you ever had a God wink come your way?
Something so unexpected and out of the blue, you were blown away?
Only believers can experience and enjoy a special nod,
And the only explanation logical is that it came from God.

When we are serving and trusting in the Lord,
The ultimate favor of blessings is constantly being poured.
How special and what joy is ours to claim,
When we are walking on the narrow path void of shame.

How can you obtain such a wink and richly receive?
By accepting Jesus as your Lord and Master and simply believe.
When God winks and gives you supernatural protection,
Be sure to give thanks and praise of exclamation.

Where Do You Find Your Hope?

Where do you find your hope?
In these tumultuous times and bending at the end of your rope.
Where do you find strength to deal with each trial you face?
And know an answer will come with God's unfailing grace.

When we are lost and every addiction and heartache keep us off course,
There is only one hope, and it is found in our perfect source.
We must keep our eyes focused on Jesus
To be certain our every prayer is answered and He sees us.

Where do you find your hope and courage to withstand duress?
To our Savior and friend, Jesus, who will break every chain and rescue us.

Who is the Captain of Your Soul?

Who is the captain of your soul?
The one and only that can save and make you whole.
Who only can lead us and provide protection
In every step we take and show direction?

The captain would be our Lord Jesus,
He alone can guide and never forsake us.
No other can show such compassion and favor
And empower us to stand against adversity as our Savior.

Who is the captain of your soul?
The one and only that can save and make you whole.
To make Jesus the captain of your soul,
Surrender completely and allow His supernatural control.

Walking in His Will

Walking daily in His will,
Can be accomplished when we listen and be still.
A strong draw to be in His grip,
To demonstrate His love and witness He will equip.

A strong conviction to be in His Word and keep on the path
Will guide our footing straight to avoid wrath.
Walking in His will is a lifetime full of merit,
So when our earthly time is over, His promises are ours to inherit.

Unfailing Love

Are you searching and yearning for an unfailing love?
A true and trusted companion that only can be found in our Savior above.
When we are rejected, abused, or depressed,
The Heavenly Father will show compassion and divinely bless.

When you search, no other source will ever satisfy,
As the one we put hope and trust in, the perfect ally!
Doesn't matter what we have done, there are no boundaries to His gift of grace;
When we surrender and follow His will, our sorrows He will replace.

Are you searching and yearning for an unfailing love?
A true and trusted companion that only can be found in our Savior above.
We should give thanks daily for this unfailing love,
As every promise and provision is fulfilled by the holy dove.

Section 2:

My Life

Go therefore and make disciples of all the nations, baptizing them in the name of the Father and of the Son and of the Holy Spirit, teaching them to observe all that I have commanded you. And behold, I am with you always, to the end of the age.

Mathew 28:19-20 (ESV)

Transformed

I thank God daily I have been transformed.
Walking in His blessing and no longer being worldly conformed.
Learning to rely strictly on His favor,
No other source or thing can compare to my Savior.

Following in His ways on the path of righteousness,
Provides more peace and joys of happiness.
A renewing of the mind and a heart meant to give
Is absolutely the will of God and way to live.

I will forever give praise for this precious gift.
Only God can provide such power and allow our spirits to lift.
I thank God daily I have been transformed.
Walking in His blessing and no longer being worldly conformed.

A Destiny with God

A power within calls me each day,
Drawing me closer than ever in the will of His way.
An awesome awareness that speaks gently to me,
Reminding me of His perfect example I want to follow faithfully.

Daily guidance to witness and be a light
Of His love and become obedient in His sight.
Promises He has given are ours to redeem,
As long as we accept Jesus as our King.

A power within calls me each day,
Drawing me closer than ever in the will of His way.
A destiny with God is one given to me by grace
That ensures that when my time here is done, I will see His face.

Soldier for God

I am called to be a soldier for God,
Armed with the equipment to march on this sod.
An assignment to witness and shine a light
To those who are lost and losing the fight.

A battle is raging, and I must stay on guard,
The weapons of attack are dark principalities that
press hard.
But I am equipped with the gear to uphold the Word
and win.
A breastplate of armor, shield of faith, and sword to
conquer sin.

A mission that will require my utmost all,
A body that is rested and rejuvenated to answer His
call.
Duty, which calls me 24/7,
Will produce power and my personal door to heaven.

I am called to be a soldier for God,
Armed with the equipment to march on this sod.
To be a soldier for God is a mission of love,
To serve in His Army will demonstrate honor to Him
above.

I Never Knew

I never knew I could find a friend so true,
One who could be so loyal and love us as no one else could ever do.
No matter what I have done or will ever do,
This one friend I can depend on, who pardons every sin, and always sees me through.

I never knew someone who could help me find a way,
To navigate my life when I feel lost by teaching me to pray.
Whenever I feel anxious or overwhelmed by fear,
There is someone who gives courage and draws ever near.

I never knew there was a book that could answer every problem of life,
A sacred book that is the divine Word of God that offers comfort and way to combat strife.
I never knew I could learn to forgive
And let bitterness go so I could have peace and no longer be a captive.

I never knew there was an internal voice

Who would provide, protect, and guide me on a
righteous course?
Marvelous miracles I have witnessed and received
From this perfect friend when I trusted and believed.

I never knew I could find a friend so true,
One who could be so loyal and love us as no one else
could ever do.
Until I found Jesus, I never knew what joy and peace
could be found
In a friend and Savior that completely turned my life
around.

A Call

God has spoken and given each life a call
To help reach others, lift, and encourage all.
To be moved by His heavenly orders
Is a duty of honor that defies all borders.

We are all given gifts which are our inheritance
To work for His kingdom and fight any pestilence.
Living in a world filled with darkness,
The mission is clear to help and save the heartless.

God has spoken and given each life a call
To help reach others, lift, and encourage all.
There is an urgency for us to respond to His call,
To be a shining light and example for all.

Heart on Fire for God

My heart is on fire for God each day
By walking in His will and listening to what He has to say.
No time to squander my life or disobey
But to follow His lead and witness every day.

There is an urgency for displaying love
To show mercy exemplified by the living dove.
A heart on fire for God is my call,
A combustible agent to encourage, uplift, and have compassion for all.

My Source

Every blessing I have comes from my heavenly source,
The one and only provider that keeps me on course.
To acknowledge and know without a doubt
Allows perfect peace and makes me witness with a shout.

Relying strictly on His everlasting arms
Brings peace and rest, fearing no harm.
My source allows me to walk daily with purpose and favor,
Jesus is my source and personal Savior.

One Life

One life we all are given
To be a blessing and heavenly driven.
The only way we will ever experience joy and peace
Is to walk righteously in love and see our blessings increase.

One life that shouldn't be wasted on the world's wrath,
But serving God and our fellow man walking on the right path.
A precious gift so fully blessed
Is ours to enjoy each moment and accept His best.

One life we all are given
To be a blessing and heavenly driven.
I have fully surrendered my one life
To stand on God's Word and avoid strife.

Who Needs Jesus?

Who needs Jesus in this life?
We all need His guidance and wisdom in a world filled with strife.
Who can bring peace and restore health,
Who can bless us with riches and wealth?

Only one can give freedom from any addiction
And bring us out of bondage and affliction.
Who can deliver us through any storm we face?
Only the perfect Messiah can grant us grace.

Who can bring peace and restore health,
Who can bless us with riches and wealth?
Only Jesus can provide a hedge of protection and eternal salvation.
Who needs Jesus? Every soul that is part of creation.

Where Else but the Lord?

Where else but the Lord should we go
When we are broken and low?
No other friend can satisfy so complete
Or can listen to our hearts and be so sweet.

Burdens, disease, stresses, and heartaches can be
relieved
When we surrender every trial and just believe.
A path that is broad, or one that is slim,
The only clear part is the one we walk with Him

No other friend can satisfy so complete
Or can listen to our hearts and be so sweet.
Where else but the Lord could we ever find more?
No other source could ever bless and completely
restore.

Heart for God

Having a heart for God is my daily goal,
To seek Him only and let Him take control.
I know my Savior searches every area of my heart,
I want to make sure I follow His direction so not to depart.

I pray daily to be a shining light,
To witness, and be an example for those battling with a fight.
Serving daily and offering my best,
No other thing can fill my heart and continue to give rest.

The Journey

The journey we must take to find victory
Is sometimes long and difficult when inheriting liberty.
The path along the road can be filled with resistance,
But the reward gained can be sought with persistence.

Wandering over mountains and valleys, God can carry us through
When we seek direction with prayer and determination and earnestly pursue.
The journey is complete when we partner with God;
Only He can provide the road which is broad.

The path along the road can be filled with resistance,
But the reward gained can be sought with persistence.
No matter where the journey leads us all,
It's worth whatever painful steps necessary to receive His call.

The Anchor of My Soul

Jesus is the anchor of my soul,
The only one source that can make me whole.
Where can I turn to find complete rest?
My Lord and Savior that only wants my best.

When troubles and turmoil of this world cause alarm,
I can turn to the one friend that protects me from any harm.
He will calm every storm and fear, leading me to a safe haven, making my way clear.

No matter how far I may drift,
He can change my course and lead me away from any rift.
Jesus is the anchor of my soul,
The only one source that can make me whole.

A Still Small Voice

A still small voice nudges me daily
To acknowledge and obey faithfully.
How can we know the voice is a godly sound?
Only when we have been saved and in His grace are found.

A voice that beckons us to make right choices;
Then and only then can we exercise righteousness.
A still small voice will be your guide,
One which will bring rest and peace in which you can abide.

Conviction

An unshakeable belief I know for sure
That God our Father is in control and is absolutely pure.
Knowing deep in my heart without a doubt
That serving our God is the highest calling and what life is all about.

A test we might face to make us break,
No wavering or uncertainty will ever allow us to shake.
No matter how long or hard the affliction,
My faith and courage will be my undying conviction.

Serving with Hearts and Hands

How should we serve our Lord according to His plan?
We should serve faithfully with our whole hearts and hands.
There is no greater allegiance and love we can display
Then to give from our hearts, let our hands assist every need, and continuously fold to pray.

As Jesus demonstrated in washing the feet of His brothers,
We are to likewise serve from our hearts and hands to others.
There is much we can do to serve and spiritually feed,
To aide countless souls and plant a hopeful seed.

Idle hands can lead to evil and make it hard to cope,
But lifting our hands to worship can provide hope.
Serving our God and fellow man is our highest call and joy,
Being mindful of the need and recognizing no injustice is too small.

When we lift our hearts and hands to serve and obey,
Our Heavenly Father will lovingly protect and guide us day to day.

Testimony for Jesus

Do you have a testimony for Jesus?
Evidence of a changed life once in pieces.
Whatever road we have traveled or mess we have made,
It is time to share our message openly and not be afraid.

Proof of a changed life allows us to give hope,
To those struggling in a storm and giving them power to cope.
Any battle or test we have been through
Is the basis for a testimony and life made new.

Proof of a changed life allows us to give hope,
To those struggling in a storm and giving them power to cope.
If we have a testimony for Jesus, take a stand,
Now is the time to gratefully acknowledge Him firsthand.

Listening to the Voice of God

Listening to the voice of God today,
As I read His Word and bow to pray.
Waiting to hear for direction before I make a move,
Knowing His almighty hand will guide me on a path
He will approve.

Listening for guidance to be in His perfect will,
Knowing where He leads, His plan will be fulfilled.
Although you may say you can't audibly hear,
When you believe and seek with all your heart, the
evidence will be crystal clear.

Today, more than ever, we must listen for the Word of
God before we act,
As signs of His return are imminent, and we must
properly react.
It is the time to make sure we are executing the great
commission
By listening and adhering to God's Word as our urgent
mission.

Section 3:

Serving God and Worship

"Let your light so shine before men, that they may see your good works and glorify your Father in heaven" (Mathew 5:16, NKJV).

Be a Light

We must strive to be a light,
To help many and exemplify what is right.
So much evil and corruption abound in the darkness
of night
That we must act with urgency and stand to fight.

For the days we are living are callous and vain,
So many souls self-absorbed, arrogant, and profane.
So many look to find the beacon of hope,
Wrestling with principalities of darkness, struggling
to cope.

We must make sure our paths are illuminated,
To ensure all destructive habits and ill will are
eliminated.
Be a light wherever you go;
So there is no doubt that all recognize the glow.

Salt and Light

We are to be salt and light in this life,
Adding taste and flavor to those struggling with strife.
To make a difference for those who hunger for
righteousness,
Quenching their thirst with faithfulness.

Just a sprinkling of seasoning to present the spirit,
So that those who witness will listen and see it.
We need to be a strong example,
Showing everyone we meet the truthful sample.

We are to be salt and light in this life,
Adding taste and flavor to those struggling with strife.
Salt and light must be shown with fervent emergency,
As the days we are living demand urgency.

Fanning the Flame

Are you fanning a flame for God?
And allowing the Holy Spirit to radiate wherever you trod?
We, as believers, are indwelled with the Holy Spirit
When we accept Jesus our Savior and supernaturally receive it.

Every good gift the Father will bestow
Can be a beacon to others of love we show.
Whatever we do with our gifts can be a witness to others
And speak life and encouragement to all our brothers.

One single spark or idea brought to mind by the spirit
Can ignite a fire to all that adherent.
To fan a flame for God will start a fire in your soul so bright
That everyone we meet will know we walk in the light.

Comrades in Christ

Comrades in Christ is what we are,
Destined to serve and shine as the brightest heavenly star.
Called each day to be in the Word and pray,
Giving us the strength and power to guide and lead others in the way.

Bound together to witness to others lost and struggling to cope,
Sharing the gospel of Jesus and giving them the true meaning of hope.
This band of brothers and sisters must continue to work vigorously,
As it is unknown how much time there is to conquer evil and win victoriously.

Comrades in Christ is what we are,
Destined to serve and shine as the brightest heavenly star.
To be a comrade in Christ, all you need is to believe,
Everything will be provided for your spirit to achieve.

Ambassadors for Christ

Are you called to be an ambassador for Christ?
A representative and disciple of Jesus who came to act as a Holy sacrifice.
All those called must put on the full armor of God,
Giving us the protection and courage to shine wherever we trod.

This important mission is urgent and clear,
Orders given to us to spread the gospel and not fear.
We are to be a beacon in a world full of darkness,
Showing God's love to everyone, especially the heartless.

To be an ambassador for Christ will require dedication and perseverance;
In these times, we are now living regardless of evil interference.
We must strive to get the message delivered of hope and goodwill
In order to help save many for the kingdom, and His mission be fulfilled.

A Servant's Spirit

Striving each day to have a servant's spirit,
One of obedience and a heart to embrace it.
A hand to reach those that may be in need,
Being available and ready to assist and spiritually feed.

A call on my life directed from above
To rescue, help, and minister to the needy with love.
A servant's spirit is one called to honor and follow his direction
To fully surrender, earnestly pray to be guaranteed supernatural protection.

Lift Up Your Voice

Lift up your voice and sing,
Give praise to the Almighty King.
Worshiping and showing adoration with our voice
Demonstrates our devotion and thankfulness by our heartfelt choice.

To sing in the choir, play an instrument, or make any joyful noise
Honors our Father and fills each one of us with an abundance of joy.
The lyre, tambourine, pipe, and trumpet—all
instruments shown to pay tribute in biblical times;
Even today still rings a melodic note so sublime.

Lift up your voice and sing as one day the final trumpet will sound,
As the earth will prepare to receive the heavenly crown.
Every angel in heaven will rejoice
When we pay respect to our Father and lift up our voice.

Worship, Walk, and Work

Worship, walk, and work are the steps to praise,
To give glory to His will and works every day.
To worship Him and give our best exaltation
Allows us to walk in His will and experience perfect salvation.

Walking entirely on His righteous path,
Will eliminate and keep us from undue wrath.
Working for the kingdom will bring glory to the King,
And walking in His ways will forever magnify and redeem.

Be a Blessing

Be a blessing today wherever you go,
Allow your heart to be so open, your love overflows.
It doesn't take much to help or reach out to one another,
A simple smile, call, or handshake can lift the spirits of a discouraged sister or brother.

Encouraging one another with kindness and shining your light,
As Jesus demonstrated giving many pure delight.
We should show humility and walk in love,
Always thinking more highly of others and putting their interests above.

It doesn't take much to help or reach out to one another,
A simple smile, call, or handshake can lift the spirits of a discouraged sister or brother.
God's greatness and favor will always be returned
Whenever you extend a helping hand to show mercy and concern.

Fruits for Life and Eternity

The fruits of the spirit flow through us naturally when
we are in Christ;
Continually being sanctified by the Holy Spirit helps
us change our sinful nature to not be wrongfully
enticed.
The nine virtues include love, joy, peace, patience,
kindness, goodness, faithfulness, gentleness, and
self-control—
These fruits show evidence that our lives are altered
and we have surrendered our souls.

All of the fruits we are given
Help make each believer grow continually and become
spiritually driven.
Although we may endure heartache, pain, and
temptation,
A certain peace and joy can be ours through constant
transformation.

Patience, kindness, and goodness we can possess no
matter our circumstances,
Our God can provide always and offer endless chances.
Faithfulness, gentleness, and self-control are virtues
that allow us to grow

Into the image of Christ through grace He freely
bestows.

All of the fruits we are given
Help make each believer grow continually and become
spiritually driven.
The fruits we enjoy each day of our life will continue
through eternity
When love indwells and we are assured of our destiny
with a certainty.

Seeking God

Aspiring to seek God each day
Allows me to be in His will and perfect way.
How can we know exactly where we can find
The answers to connect with God and have peace of mind?

Calling out to God in heartfelt prayer
And diligently pursuing will yield a response after asking and surrendering.
Studying the Word and yearning for direction
Will enlighten our part and give us perfect instruction.

Aspiring to seek God each day
Allows me to be in His will and perfect way.
Seeking God each day when I rise
Renews my faith before my eyes.

Running My Race

A call to run my race
And follow His direction and adjust my pace.
Wherever His route should lead,
I will pursue and follow with speed.

I will keep the faith and finish the course
Knowing that I am in God's will and proceed with a
steady force.
No distraction or deterrent will slow me down,
Knowing at the end I will receive the victor's crown.

I will keep the faith and finish the course
Knowing that I am in God's will and proceed with a
steady force.
"Well done, good and faithful servant—" are the words
I long to hear
When my race is finished and my time is over here.

Don't Give Up

Don't ever give up on whatever trial you face,
Keep fighting and believing that God will bring you into a better place.
Although times may seem dark and there is no hope,
Our breakthrough is closer than we know, and God will equip us to cope.

Don't ever give up on whatever trial you face,
Keep fighting and believing that God will bring you into a better place.
When the road is long and our faith is brought to the test,
God will make a way and deliver His very best.

Don't ever give up on whatever trial you face,
Keep fighting and believing that God will bring you into a better place.
Keep fighting and never give up although you are worn down,
For at the end of your battle you will be awarded a victor's crown.

Section 4: Salvation

"For by grace you have been saved through faith, and that not of yourselves; it is the gift of God, not of works, lest anyone should boast" (Ephesians 2:8-9, NKJV).

Come to the Cross

When you are overwhelmed and filled with loss,
That is the beckoning invitation to come to the cross.
Burdens so unimaginable to endure and withstand
Will be lifted and relieved by His power and hand.

All of the suffering, pain, and disgrace
Can be completely abandoned and simply erased.
Our Savior paid the ultimate price
When He hung there to redeem and sacrifice.

Yes, our Savior paid the ultimate price
When He hung there to redeem and sacrifice.
All the suffering, misery, and drops of blood He shed,
Where we no longer experience death but eternal life instead.

Eternal Salvation

An eternal salvation is ours when we are born again.
Joint heirs with God when we confess our sin to Him.
A process that is one we must make
In order to inherit promises that are ours to partake.

Confessing our sin, asking for forgiveness, and inviting Jesus into our heart
Are the steps to allow us to experience a brand new start.
Jesus' resurrection broke each heavy chain,
He freed us from bondage and erased every guilty stain.

Rescued

I have been rescued and set free
From a drowning sea of distress and misery.
Overwhelmed by an undertow of doubt and despair,
When miraculously, my Heavenly Father reached
down and saved me from a snare.

Time and time again I was consumed with waves of
fear
Until I found the ultimate source that would take back
the wheel to steer.
I now have found an anchor that I can embrace,
As I am safe and secure by His amazing grace.

No longer drifting and lost in a raging sea,
I can rejoice knowing God has delivered and rescued
me.
Whatever storm you may be going through,
Put your trust in Jehovah God, and He will protect and
rescue you.

Broken

When all of our being has been bent and broken,
This is the time we must yield and hear what is spoken.
No one can mend the shattered parts
Like our Heavenly Father who heals each and every responsive heart.

Although we feel overwhelmed with grief and defeat,
The answer God reveals is trustworthy and complete.
Just simply because God sacrificed and offered His Son as a token,
We can be assured of salvation and completely forgiven when broken.

Out of the Darkness

There is a way to move out of the darkness,
And that is by accepting a Savior that opens our eyes to
a new brightness.
No longer must we remain in bitterness,
unforgiveness, and blame,
But we can walk in a light that will allow us to embrace
life with no shame.

We can be washed clean from every dirty stain,
From a rescuer that will release us from all the heavy
chains.
Every addiction, stronghold, or feeling of loss
Can be wiped away completely at the foot of the cross.

When we wander over the same mountains trying to
cope,
There is a perfect assurance of a helper who will lend a
hand of hope.
What a joy and sense of peace when we surrender and
step out of the darkness,
For we now have gained an eternal life that provides
everlasting luminescence.

To Forgive

To forgive is a decision we all must make
Not to continue to blame, criticize, or forsake.
To drop the offense and forget the injustice
Is an act so compassionate we can erase the wrong done to us.

To forgive is a decision we all must make
Not to continue to blame, criticize, or forsake.
Even though the pain can be so strong,
To forgive frees us to continue to move on.

To forgive is a decision we all must make
Not to continue to blame, criticize, or forsake.
Through God's love, we can learn this deed;
By His example and His death, He planted the seed.

To forgive is a decision we all must make
Not to continue to blame, criticize, or forsake.
To forgive is a justification and cleansing act,
One that will bring victory and healing back.

The Time for Redemption

The time for redemption is now.
A time to look up, fold our hands to pray, and mercifully bow.
A time of searching for answers to these uncertain times,
Watching a world filled with fear, anarchy, and immense crime.

So many wrestling with depression, despair, and questions on how to cope,
Unaware, there is only one response to our search for eternal hope.
Many signs we are observing the "End of Age,"
Where lawlessness abounds, pestilence, betrayal, and hatred rage.

We are being given an opportunity to secure our salvation,
A chance to turn from our iniquities and guarantee our vindication.
Confessing we are sinners, belief in the gospel, and making Jesus Lord
Are the sincere steps we must make to be restored.

The time for redemption is now.
A time to look up, fold our hands to pray, and
mercifully bow.
There is an urgency that requires our immediate
attention;
Now is the "Time for Redemption."

Desperation

Sometimes, we only seek God's Word in desperation
When everything we try to do fills us with
exasperation.
If we seek Him, and only Him first,
The meditation and prayer focused through Him will
quench every thirst.

So much pain and burdens can be relieved,
If we search and earnestly seek to receive
Let us not wait until our only time is desperation
But seeking Him always to find comfort and
restoration.

Decision

Are you on the brink of making a decision?
Straddling on the fence of life, headed on a path of collision.?
We all must make that one definitive course of action
And think clearly where our eternal destiny lies to find complete satisfaction.

There is an urgency to make this choice of either life or death,
Individually choosing how we spend each minute, and prayerfully thankful for our every breath.
Eternal life is available to all who believe
If you are willing to confess, repent, and just receive.

If you are on the brink of making a decision,
You are straddling the fence of life, headed for a path of collision.
A desire to walk in the light and experience a spiritual vision
Will bring peace and joy and manifest a straightforward decision.

Rejected

There is deep pain when we are rejected,
When those we trusted and love leave us sad and neglected.
Although we can allow ourselves to hold onto the torment and disbelief,
We can release the burden by letting our Heavenly Father deliver relief.

No other promise is so reassuring to know that He will never forsake us or leave,
Trusting in Him completely when we believe.
Whatever amount of hatred or negativity we are dealt,
It can diminish when the calmness and assurance are supernaturally felt.

Oh, there is deep pain when we are rejected,
When those we trusted and love leave us sad and neglected.
But to look to our Heavenly Father and have the hurt erased
Will be the answer we seek when He offers His unconditional grace.

Drifting

Are you in danger of drifting and pulling away
From the only true source that can provide a way?
Walking on a path that is rebellious and out of the Father's will
Can only bring disillusionment, pain, sorrow, and ill will.
Like a drifting ship into the sea,
Turning back to our faithful anchor can bring victory.
Two important instruments that are essential to avoid drifting
Are prayer and being in the Word daily to aid in the process of sifting.

Are you in danger of drifting and pulling away
From the only true source that can provide a way?
It is time to get back on course and rebuild a strong foundation,
A time to ensure drifting is erased from future generations.

Last Resort

Our first choice when we need God's support
Often comes as an action of last resort.
If only we will trust in God's perfect way,
So much heartache can be relieved when we pray.

In our own strength, nothing can be solved,
Leaning on the Word and power can our problems be resolved.
To gain God's power when we continue to ignore and neglect
Will only cause needless worry and regret.

In our own strength, nothing can be solved,
Leaning on the Word and power can our problems be resolved.
So let's not make prayer our last resort,
But pray before problems arise and find our comfort.

Stars for Scars

When we are in the valley and feeling battered and covered with scars,
The very moment when we ask God, He will provide a light to witness stars.
Although we may be confused and unable to reason,
God can turn around any trial and put us in a new season.

We are promised a heavenly crown, and I believe it is filled with stars;
When we live the life of God's purpose, He will erase away the scars.
So to be His child and live according to His will,
We must take up our cross and wait for the voice ever so still.

Although we may be confused and unable to reason,
God can turn around any trial and put us in a new season.
Only by being redeemed can we ever witness the heavenly stars,
But how great our reward when relieved of all our scars.

Rescued and Redeemed

No matter how far you have drifted or how lost your life may seem,
You can be totally rescued and redeemed.
When we falter into a pit and total darkness is all we can see,
We can call on our Heavenly Father to shine a light to set us free.

Traveling down the wide road holds much attraction and allure,
Only the narrow road provides a rescuing hand and eternal care.
For every feeling of guilt, shame, or remorse,
Each chain of bondage can be broken when we submit to the heavenly voice.

While on the mountaintop, life can seem ecstatic and serene,
But only in the valley do you realize your need for a rescuer and to be redeemed.
Today is the time to turn away from darkness and become highly esteemed;
When we surrender and transform to be rescued and redeemed.

The Lamb's Book of Life

Is your name written in the Lamb's Book?
God's everlasting book that ensures that all that have
been saved will never be overlooked?
How can we know we are guaranteed this reservation?
Only when we have accepted Jesus as our personal
Savior and experience transformation.

No amount of good works will ever qualify,
Only being born again will completely justify.
Once your name has been written,
Nothing can erase the fact you are interminably
forgiven.

God has promised every believer this special gift of
reserve,
A holy inscription that is endlessly preserved.
To be written in The Lamb's Book offers a peace that
assures
That our souls are forever secure.

An Encounter with Jesus

Have you experienced an encounter with Jesus,
The only source that can rescue, redeem, and restore us?
An encounter with Jesus will relieve any uncertainty;
To be in the presence of Jesus secures your eternity.

Whatever bondage, addiction, or pain we endure, He will deliver;
The shield, comfort, and peace can be yours from the giver.
He can meet us wherever we are;
There is never any distance too far.

No encounter is purely circumvention;
Make no mistake, it is divine intervention.
An encounter with Jesus will relieve any uncertainty;
To be in the presence of Jesus secures your eternity.

Highway to Heaven

Are you on the highway to heaven roadway,
Striving to reach the kingdom of God today?
Although there are rocky roads and curves to steer clear of,
The reward of choosing this path is unconditional love.

Many will begin this highway and fall off the course,
But those that stand strong will continue with supernatural force.
We must keep on a steady track,
Looking straight ahead, not wavering or looking back.

If we should suddenly falter or become lost,
The main road sign to seek in the cross.
So set your GPS with the voice of Jesus,
Knowing this voice will never mislead us.

So are you on the highway to heaven roadway,
Striving to reach the kingdom of God today?
We can be sure with complete certainty
That the highway to heaven will safeguard our eternity.

Divine Intervention

Have you experienced a divine intervention?
A direct involvement of goodness with a virtuous intention?
It can happen to any believer that has faith and will earnestly pray;
A spiritual intercession that can work miracles any moment of the day.

I have witnessed and am of the strong conviction
That our faithful God will lead us and change any wrong direction.
Angels stand by us to guard and protect,
Remaining steadfast until ordered to project.

Only as believers can this phenomenon occur,
And with complete trust will our hope be assured.
The promise of divine intervention can be yours and mine today
If you are willing to rely solely on His direction without delay.

GPS (Great Personal Savior)

Do you have a GPS (Great Personal Savior)?
One who can give you solid direction and ultimate favor?
If you are faltering and can't find a way,
The GPS will come and rescue you if you invite Him in today.

There are only two roads we can travel,
The narrow and the broad way, where the broad will allow us to disconnect and unravel.
Entering the narrow road can provide peace and virtuousness,
Leading us in His perfect will and righteousness.

So if you are faltering and can't find a way,
The GPS will come and rescue you if you invite Him in today.
We are all in need of the GPS as our compass
Where we can be assured of the guidance of Jesus for us.

Born Again

How can we be born again?
By receiving Christ and accepting the everlasting gift bestowed to all men.
We must put away all our fleshly desires
In order to inherit the righteousness of heaven and avoid the eternal fires.

A spiritual rebirth occurs when our hearts are transformed;
No more walking in the ways of the world, confused and misinformed.
To be assured of seeing God and His kingdom,
One must be born of water and the spirit to be guaranteed freedom.

How can we be born again?
By receiving Christ and accepting the everlasting gift bestowed to all men.
To have a relationship with Jesus should be the ultimate aim for all men
To be certain sin has been forgiven and know we are born again.

Section 5: Holidays

"One person esteems one day as better than another, while another esteems all days alike. Each day should be fully convinced in his own mind" (Romans 14:5, ESV).

St. Patrick's Day

We commemorate March 17th as the day
St. Patrick brought Christianity to Ireland and paved the way.
Born in Roman Britain and kidnapped as a teen from his native land,
He was brought to become a slave to tend sheep in Slemish Mountain, Ireland.

After spending six years there dealing with paganism and slavery,
He fled his master and returned to Britain from captivity.
Following his return, a call from the Lord would beckon him to return to Ireland;
To journey far and wide baptizing and confirming many under the direction of God's hand.

According to legend, a shamrock was used by St. Patrick to explain the Holy Trinity;
Today it remains a symbol of all things Irish: and the Father, Son, and Holy Ghost; the complete Divinity.
Many festivities are associated with St. Patrick's Day:
Parades, special foods, wearing of the green, Irish dance, and music played.

St. Patrick today is honored in many lands,
As the saint that spread the gospel and allowed many to understand.
So we commemorate March 17th as the day
Because St. Patrick brought Christianity to Ireland and paved the way.

The Miracle Of Easter

The miracle of Easter is the promise of new birth
When our Lord Jesus Christ died, was resurrected, and gave us all a sense of worth.
Palm Sunday, the Sunday prior to Easter, is known as the start of Holy Week
Where Christians around the world reflect and diligently seek.

Many traditions are associated with this important holiday:
Coloring and hiding eggs, the Easter bunny, parades, and decorated bonnets—all a popular mainstay.
The Easter lily, which is a mark of purity and innocence,
Embellishes churches and homes on this day representing holy reverence.

It is the season of new beginning, of flowers abloom, animals awakening and eagerly anticipating the celebration of spring.
The time to plant seed, smell of new green grass, and hearing the sweetness of the robin sing.
So many customs are associated and practiced on this most holy day.

The most significant marvel is the fact that Jesus died
on a cross to take all our sins away.

The miracle of Easter is the promise of new birth
When our Lord Jesus Christ died, was resurrected, and
gave us all a sense of worth.
The miracle of Easter can be witnessed every day.
When we surrender our lives to the living God and
strive to obey.

Blessings of Motherhood

Being a mother is one of God's highest callings and
anointed favor;
To be entrusted with this responsibility is bestowed by
our Heavenly Savior.
A role that requires much nurturing and teaching,
But the rewards are lasting and far-reaching.

To train up our children in the way they must go
Will instill values that allow them to develop and
spiritually grow.
Empathy, patience, and love are just a few of the
qualities of dedicated motherhood;
Demonstrating acts of sacrifice, endurance, and
humility show affectionate servanthood.

To fulfill the duty as a mother is beyond measure,
And the pride experienced is a priceless treasure.
We should honor and love our mothers with tender
emotion,
To pay respect and reverence with unconditional
devotion.

Instructing and disciplining to make the wise choice,

Taught from the Good Book with guidance from the
heavenly voice.
May the blessings of motherhood give you
contentment and joy,
Knowing you were God's instrument in mentoring
each girl and boy.

Memorial Day

Originally called Decoration Day and proclaimed in 1868,
Memorial Day was first observed on the May 30th date.
It was first marked as a day to remember our fallen heroes
Although today, many have forgotten the true meaning of honoring those.

A tradition of wearing a red poppy in honor of those dying during World War I was begun;
Since 1922, the VFW sells poppies in hope many will wear one.
A national moment of remembrance was passed in 2000 to honor and observe;
Asking that at 0300 local time, Americans stop to pay a moment of silence to those that deserve.

For every serviceman and servicewoman that answered the call,
Please let's remember and never forget those that paid it all.

What Is a Dad?

A dad is a man who will guide you with a firm hand,
He will encourage you to begin to walk until you finally stand.
He will be there to show you how to ride a bike or play ball
And rush to your side if you stumble and fall.

A dad will teach you to use a hammer or learn a skill,
Helping you with homework or assisting mom to make you a special meal.
As you grow, he will help you to have courage and be strong
And to be humble with principles to keep you from doing wrong.

A dad, who demonstrates love to your mom and you and can kneel to pray,
Will be a guiding light you will remember and honor all your days.

Independence Day

A day all Americans should cherish and appreciate
Is one filled with parades and fireworks we excitedly celebrate.
We should thank God for our unique Independence Day
And be on guard to ensure it is never taken away.

In 1776, our forefathers signed and guaranteed our inalienable rights,
A nation built on principle many have defended with a continual fight.
We should thank God for our unique Independence Day
And be on guard to ensure it is never taken away.

A flag that stands for justice and equality
No other country can compare to its character and quality.
We should thank God for our unique Independence Day
And be on guard to ensure it is never taken away.

Pride is the emotion that fills the night skies
Each July 4th with beauty bursting before our eyes.
We should thank God for our unique Independence Day
And be on guard to ensure it is never taken away.

Veteran's Day

Thank you, Mr. And Ms. Veteran, on this Veterans Day.
Your sacrifice and dedication we note, and a great debt we pay.
First observed on the 11th hour of the 11th day and 11th month of 1918,
Then called Armistice Day after the end of World War I, a proclamation was seen.

A day set aside to celebrate and honor all who serve for their love of country and patriotism.
And bring to remembrances each serviceman's selfless heroism.
Marked by parades, church services, and in many places, flags flown at half-mast.
This day has paid tribute to many and hopefully will always bring recognition of those servicemen from today and the past.

Whenever there is despotism or peril in our land,
It is the courageous and faithful veteran that will always fight for freedom and take a stand.
Every time you see a veteran on this special day,
Remember to give a special salute and a handshake of gratefulness to take away.

Right of Freedom

A right of freedom we should voice
When it comes to deciding our favorite choice.
In early November, please make a note
To go to the polls and cast your vote.

No matter your party affiliation,
Take time to make your decision.
In early November, please make a note
To go to the polls and cast your vote.

Casting a ballot in this election
Ensures your candidate moves in the right direction.
In early November, please make a note
To go to the polls and cast your vote.

This right of freedom to which we are blessed
Is found in our country, the very best.
In early November, please make a note
To go to the polls and cast your vote.

A Time to Be Thankful

A time to be thankful for all the joys we have been
blest,
A time to pause, meditate, and take time to rest.
A time to give thanks to God above
For family and friends that surround us with love.

Favorite traditions we observe in the fall
Reflecting on memories of food, parades, and football.
A time to be mindful of those serving on the line,
So we can happily wine and dine.

Lest we forget the sacrifices they endure
To make sure our freedom is insured.
A time to be thankful should occur each and every day
To be grateful for a country where we can be free and
pray.

Miracle of Christmas

What is this miracle of Christmas we celebrate every
December?
A miraculous birth of the King of Kings we reverently
remember.
Biblical prophecy foretold of a Messiah that many
hearts hoped for and awaited to receive;
But today, as in those days, many hearts are hardened
and refuse to believe.

The angel Gabriel visited Mary, and to her expectancy
news he would bring;
She would become the virgin mother of Jesus, our
King of Kings.
This baby would be born in a manger in Bethlehem
Where shepherds and wise men would follow a bright
star to bring gifts and adoration to Him.

The significance of the baby Jesus' birth
Demonstrates the humility and servanthood God
manifested to earth.
God's purpose was straightforward and clear
To save mankind from sin and redeem all, far and
near.

Today as we once more prepare to celebrate the
miracle of Christmas
Let us remember the true meaning and be a light to
witness.

New Year's Wishes

New Year's wishes being sent your way
As we prepare to celebrate the year's first day.
From east to west celebrations will be seen,
As Father Time marches out in rapid stream.

The countdown will begin with noisemakers and light,
With champagne uncorking and a kiss at midnight.
As we ring in the New Year with "Auld Lang Syne,"
Thoughts of new resolutions will start to unwind.

New Year's wishes of health and happiness
Fill our hearts with the promise of gladness.
New Year's wishes being sent your way
As we prepare to celebrate the year's first day.

Section 6:
World in Crisis

For nation will rise against nation, and kingdom against kingdom. And there will be famines, pestilences, and earthquakes in various places. All these are the beginnings of sorrows. Then they will deliver you up to tribulation and kill you, and you will be hated by all nations for My name's sake.

Mathew 24:7-9 (NKJV)

Invisible Enemy

(Coronavirus Pandemic)
An invisible enemy has invaded our land.
Taking on men, women, and children in many
countries with proportions hard to understand.
A virus that attacks without respect of person,
Gripping a body with flu-like symptoms that can
develop and worsen.

A disease that began in China and swiftly moved west,
Striking many countries until moving to our nation,
causing panic and distress.
Is this a prophetic sign or a definitive plea
To beckon us all to redemption and fall on our knees?

This Coronavirus, we all are now facing, is epidemic,
Now defined as an infectious "global pandemic."
We are now being told to stay home and quarantine,
So we are repeatedly practicing good hygiene, social
distancing, and keeping our hands clean.

So many first responders working tirelessly day and
night
Trying to save lives, sometimes without essential PPE,
to win the fight.

There are no answers to how long this pandemic may remain,
So we must continue to follow guidelines and diligently sustain.

May we all look to the Lord for provision and hope,
As we bond together to persevere and cope.
Let's continue to pray and seek help from above
And unite cooperatively with strength, courage, and unconditional love.

A Rising Up

A rising up is being seen and felt all across this nation,
A reaction to hatred, murder, and racism by a restless generation.
What is the answer to these outcries of rioting, violence, and protests?
It must be a Christ-like behavior, only our Savior can fully demonstrate best.

Fighting evil with evil will never satisfy,
Only responding with a peaceful heart and gentleness of spirit will reunify.
A nation divided must be reconciled with an outpouring of prayer
To bond our brothers and sisters from the depths of despair.

It is time to stop this anarchy and unrest and find a way
To pave a path of forgiveness and solidarity today.
We must humbly bow to our Creator for an answer to combat this oppression,
With a sincere and prayerful heart for God to heal our broken land with His divine intercession.

Why?

Why I ask myself each day,
Are so many people turning away?
Walking on a road of destruction and hate
With no direction, purpose, or inclination of fate?

Why do they not listen to the "still small voice"?
Which calls each one of us to make the right choice?
So many are pulling away from their only hope,
Ignoring our Father's Word, seemingly not knowing
how to cope.

Why do they ignore and discount
That each evil deed will be judged when we one day
give account?
Why do I not fully understand?
What has happened to our society and the heart of
man?

Why I ask myself each day,
Why are so many people turning away?
There is only one answer to restore and heal today—
To repent, ask for forgiveness, kneel and pray.

Path of Destruction

(Moore, Oklahoma–May 2013)

A path of destruction has shown its wrath,
As an EF-5 tornado hit hard in Oklahoma and marked its path.
An entire town in despair and disarray
While so many first responders try to help and clear a way.

So much heartbreak and emotional duress
Is evident in the aftermath with many signs of hopelessness.
An elementary school took the hardest heavy toll,
As many small children lost their precious souls.

Although what looks unrepairable and damaged at unimaginable cost,
Some goodness will prevail in the heroic deeds that are for those who have lost.
Out of the ashes, many will rebuild and rise,
As God will provide comfort and place a rainbow in the skies.

Stand

It is time to take a stand
For what is right and just in our land.
We cannot conform to this world and be immuned
But rather have the courage to speak up and act soon.

The spiritual fruits we strive to possess
Will give us the strength to stand up under duress.
Evil and deception are battling all around,
It's time to get prepared and stand our ground.

It is time to take a stand
For what is right and just in our land.
Taking a stand will require much from each;
It's not too late, so let's work diligently and beseech.

Sandy

(Hurricane Sandy–October 2012)

A hurricane with unmatchable devastation and force
Has been unleashed and sent it on a catastrophic course.
Brewing in the Atlantic, its surge began,
Showing its mighty force in the northeast part of our land.

Moving west and leaving blizzard conditions,
Many were unprepared and left with no provisions.
Mass flooding and destruction in the northeast shore
Left many homeless and in array as never felt before.

Its destructive track killed across eight counties, leaving much damage and misery;
Superstorm Sandy will be remembered as one of the most destructive storms in US history.

Tragedy in Florida

(Parkland, Florida–February 14th, 2018)

Another senseless day of terror and madness,
Leaving so many students, teachers, and parents with extreme sadness.
This time the crime happened in Florida State
Where the suspect accused apparently was disturbed and filled with hate.

Time and time again, our media unfolds these horrific scenes right before our eyes,
As we are overwhelmed with grief and the outburst of somber cries.
Now is the time to come together and pray
For all those affected on this heartbreaking day.

What is the solution to stop this insanity?
We must all take a stand to save humanity.
Dispelling God from our schools and public places,
Most certainly left a void and caused displacement.

Now is the time to come together and pray
For all those affected on this heartbreaking day.
Although so much needs to be answered and we continue to look,
One solution that seems logical is to turn back to the Good Book.

When the World Is Crumbling

When the world seems to be crumbling all around,
There is one source we can rely on and know that a perfect peace can be found.
So much corruption, deception, and evil is on the rise;
How can we escape and shut out every vicious act from our eyes?

Turning away and ignoring our only hope in a crumbling world today
Results in pride, lack of compassion, and a neglectful heart, unwilling to pray.
Submitting ourselves with a humble will and a desire to make a change,
Can calm every anxiety and provide a divine exchange

When catastrophic events seem overwhelming and doomsday seems at hand,
We can be assured that all believers in Christ will remain unshakable and stand.
Experiencing joy and being at rest when the world is crumbling,
Only can happen when we choose to call on God and avert further stumbling.

Terrible Tuesday

(September 11th, 2011)

911 was the call and the date
When so many lives met their fate.
Who would have thought such a crime
Could have happened here in our time?

The world trade center hit by hijacked planes,
And a part of the pentagon zapped in vain.
A downed plane headed by evil foes,
Averted targets by brave everyday heroes.

Police and firefighters working around the clock
Trying to rescue and help, dealing with shock.
Sights too horrific to comprehend,
But eyes still focused until the end.

Freedom will ever be a part of this story,
As American hearts are bonded by "Old Glory."
May God bless our land from terrorism
And keep the American spirit alive with patriotism.

Terrible Tuesday will remain heavy in our hearts,
But the spirit of liberty can never depart.

Section 7:
Biblical Findings

"Your word is a lamp to my feet and a light to my path" (Psalms 119:105, NKJV).

The Book

Are you searching for answers to life, not knowing
where to look?
There is only one reference of information that will
give guidance;
And that is the good book.

For every problem and trial we will ever face,
Try opening the pages that will provide comfort and
grace.
A book that is filled with promises you can always
trust,
From one promiser that is loyal and just.

A complete guide on how to live,
Defining our purpose and the ways we should strive to
give.
A book filled with stories of love, hope, faith, and
redemption,
And the answer to eternal salvation.

The complete biography of our "one perfect Savior"
And how He came to rescue mankind and exemplify
perfect behavior.
A bestselling book of all time
Is the "Holy Bible," and we should cherish it our entire
lifetime.

Obeying God

Obeying God is the commandment that is an absolute must;
To honor Him, surrender, and receive blessings when we trust.
To follow and listen completely to His direction
Will provide an abundance of joy and shield of protection.

Taking small steps of faith that we may not understand,
But walking in His will, we can realize our purpose in His plan.
Obeying God is the only way
To enjoy a life of peace and happiness every day.

Unconditional Promises

Do you know there are many promises just for you?
Unconditional promises that are ours eternally,
sacred, and true.
When we are reborn and walking with Jesus,
So many promises we can claim and be assured of His
faithfulness.

Promises of healing and being restored to health,
Supplying many blessings for prosperity and wealth.
A pledge to protect all from fear when we sleep,
Realizing a sense of peace from a sincere vow only He
can keep.

Provision for a hedge of protection,
Trusting we are covered in every direction.
The greatest promise of all—John 3:16—Secures our
eternal destiny and represents God's greatest love;
Ours to inherit when we repent and submit to our
Heavenly Father above.

The Shepherd's Promise

The Shepherd's promises are reliable and true;
Promises so faithful and comforting, they always provide for you.
A promiser whose character is so steadfast and unfailing,
You can bank on every promise to be prevailing.

Like the sheep who have lost their way,
Our heavenly Shepherd will keep His eye on each and not allow us to stray.
When we are in the flood or the fire,
His promise to never leave or forsake us will lift us from the mire.

In times of turbulence and trials when it is hard to stand,
The Shepherd of all consolation will firmly hold our hand.
Seeking strength and shelter for every battle we face,
A refuge will be bestowed from His continuous grace.

Our everlasting peace and eternal salvation
Is assured when our footing is on His foundation.
Promised to be blessed wherever we go
When we obey His law and diligently follow.

The Shepherd's promise will supply every need and
want if you simply believe;
Promises to claim for your own when you receive.

Child of God

A child of God is whosoever will call upon His name,
Repent sincerely to be cleansed and held without blame.
No other relationship will ever compare or offer rest
Than that of our eternal Father's best.

What a privilege and honor to know in your heart
You are a member of God's royal family and can never depart.
Although we won't be perfect and will occasionally sin,
The power of the blood will restore any iniquity, and we can win.

No other relationship will ever compare or offer rest
Than that of our eternal Father's best.
Every promise of God is ours to claim
When we are His children purchased with the blood and liberated from shame.

Discernment

A knowing in our spirit that is supernaturally placed;
A realization of knowledge only believers can embrace.
A still small voice that allows us to be aware
Of what the natural man can never understand or
care.

A blessing that is bestowed as a miraculous vision
To all those that accepted Christ and made Him their
personal decision.
When situations arise and not certain where to turn,
Prayer and faith will empower us to discern.

A still small voice that allows us to be aware
Of what the natural man can never understand or
care.
I thank God daily for the gift of discernment,
As it allows me to walk in understanding and
refinement.

Shine

We are instructed to be an example and to shine
In a world of darkness that has become blind.
Mercy and grace are God-given gifts
That are bestowed upon us to extend and lift.

The light that is seen comes from deep down
And produces a gleam when others are around.
The Holy Spirit that lives on the inside
Is the source of power we are unable to hide.

We are instructed to be an example and to shine
In a world of darkness that has become blind.
To shine for Jesus is living life at its best
In order to have peace and be able to rest.

Peacemaker

Do you know the ultimate peacemaker,
The one who removes all our anxiety and is our compassionate caregiver?
When we are burdened by trials that are unimaginable,
He alone can restore a calmness that is unshakable.

The only one who can bring complete serenity
In the turbulence of any storm and provide perfect tranquility.
Striving to be a peacemaker can bring blessings to others,
Delivering empathy and removing strife to our sisters and brothers.

Importance of Prayer

How much time do you take to pray?
Talking to our Heavenly Father and telling Him all we need to say?
Every need and request should be spoken and laid at His feet;
Expecting if the request we seek is in His will, He will complete.

Communing with God is a great privilege and gift,
An anchor in good and bad times enabling us not to drift.
He commands His children to come to Him and pray
Conversing and acknowledging everything to Him every day.

Not only does He command and expect our prayers
But wants to answer our every petition whenever we cast our cares.
The importance of prayer is essential to every believer
Knowing God will provide an answer to each receiver.

Answered Prayers

Through the trials and times of tears,
Only one God can answer every prayer and conquer all fears.
Trusting and relying completely on the truth of His Word,
Knowing each promise can never be broken or blurred.

Believing with all your heart and offering every hope in prayer
Can overcome all anxiety, leaving each worry in His tender care.
Fighting every battle on our knees that we must face,
Only through prayer and God's unfailing love bestows grace.

Answered prayer is God's response to obedience and demonstration of ultimate favor
When we release every uncertainty upon the Heavenly Savior.
No matter the circumstance or the depth of despair
When two or more agree on earth as touching anything they shall ask,
There can be the miracle of "Answered Prayer."

A Mighty God We Serve

What a Mighty God we serve,
One who offers countless blessings and favor even when we don't deserve.
When in the valleys, desperation and hopelessness can make our lives look bleak;
This is the time to focus our eyes completely on Jesus, and His will we must seek.

Whatever situation we are facing in our life, and when things look dire,
We must stay strong and not fear as our Mighty God will carry us through every flame and fire.
His almighty power and supernatural wonder seem almost a mystery;
But when we lean not on our own understanding, He will always lead us to victory.

What a Mighty God we serve,
One who offers countless blessings and favor even when we don't deserve.
I give praise and thanks each day to our Mighty God for every breath
For He alone will conquer every worry and allow us to overcome death.

Good Fruit

Are you demonstrating the qualities of good fruit?
Allowing those around us to see your virtue and never
have reason to dispute?
Good Fruits of kindness, gentleness, and love—
Just a few characteristics of the spirits that are
provided from above.

Learning to develop and display each fruit willingly
Will yield lasting treasures in eternity.
Whenever the Holy Spirit comes to dwell within,
We are assured that each good fruit will override sin.

Are you demonstrating the qualities of good fruit?
Allowing those around us to see your virtue and never
have reason to dispute?
Exhibiting the evidence daily of good fruit
Will leave no question of your foundational root.

Section 8:

Tributes and Memorials

"My command is this: Love each other as I have loved you. Greater love has no one than this: to lay down one's life for one's friends" (John 15:12-13, NIV).

Heaven Sent

(Dedicated to Livia)

God provided a heaven-sent friend,
One of God's purposely placed angels sent to bless and defend.
Although our paths had crossed in the past,
God's chosen timing would serve a bond to last.

This chosen heaven-sent friend
Is one of God's purposely placed angels sent to bless and defend.
A woman of God, whose faith is so strong,
Was placed in my life to confirm where and to whom I belong.

This chosen heaven-sent friend
Is one of God's purposely placed angels sent to bless and defend.
Sparkles and sunshine are the qualities she shows,
Such a special light that always glows.

This chosen heaven-sent friend
Is one of God's purposely placed angels sent to bless and defend.
A heaven-sent friend for whom I thank God above;
This priceless treasure I will cherish and love.

A Tribute to a Friend

(Dedicated to Jack)

As we remember fondly a special man,
We will always smile when we think of his unique brand.
An army career would be his occupation of choice;
The military police branch would ultimately convey his voice.
A protocol officer would be his specialty,
Allowing many the chance to witness his creativity.

As we remember fondly this special man,
We will always smile when we think of his unique brand.
His love and compassion for animals was beyond devotion:
Caring for his four-legged companions with heartfelt emotion.

As we remember fondly this special man,
We will always smile when we think of his unique brand.
Golf was the game that made him strive
To practice and search for the perfectly straight drive.
Sharing twenty-six years with his dedicated wife,
She took special care and added so much to his life.

As we remember fondly this special man,
We will always smile when we think of his unique brand.
A friend that will really never depart,
For he will live forever in our hearts.

A Soldier's Promotion

(Dedicated to Chaplain Gramling)

One of God's humble soldiers is being recognized today
As a promotion ceremony, giving glory to God renders cachet.
A faithful Army Chaplain for fourteen years
Has served God and country with many hours of blood, sweat, and tears.

A special calling to the army has led him to provide much inspiration to others,
Teaching and mentoring lessons of faith to countless sisters and brothers.
Many assignments, including Kentucky, North and South Carolina, Germany, and Iraq
Gave him the opportunity to spread the gospel and guide his appointed flock.

His loving family has stood by faithfully,
Also serving and making a difference wherever joyfully.
So we praise God for this blessing and lift our hands in prayer and gratitude,
As our faithful Army Chaplain is promoted today and continues to practice servitude.

A Beautiful New Granddaughter

(Dedicated to Ashlynn)

A beautiful new granddaughter has just arrived,
Filling our hearts with so much pride.
A miracle, wrapped in pink and adorned with bows,
Will be loved greatly and cherished as she grows.

A beautiful new granddaughter has just arrived,
Filling our hearts with so much pride.
Two older brothers are eager to hold and protect,
And doting family members making sure there is no
neglect.

A beautiful new granddaughter has just arrived,
Filling our hearts with so much pride.
A precious gift God sent for a specific plan
To be nurtured and guided by His hand.

This baby girl is a blessing ever so sweet
To add a special charm and sparkle to complete.
Filling our hearts with so much pride,
A beautiful new granddaughter has just arrived.

Retirement Day

(Dedicated to Chaplain Young)

Retirement day has finally arrived
For a special family with great excitement and pride.
A devout man, who has served God and country faithfully,
Now will pursue other interests with God's will diligently.

Serving as an Army Chaplain with the unique gift to preach,
His divine messages and sermons have touched many and far reached.
His loving and dedicated family have stood by faithfully,
Also serving and making a difference wherever joyfully.

Retirement day has finally arrived
For a special family with great excitement and pride.
His loving and dedicated family have stood by faithfully,
Also serving and making a difference wherever joyfully.

No other profession could be more honorable and
worthy of praise
As to serve this great country in these perilous days.
Few families, I have been privileged to know,
exemplify and shine
Like this family of God that has faithfully served ever
so sublime.

Seventy Sensational Years

(Dedicated to Terry)

Today we gather to celebrate seventy sensational years—
A life well lived—filled with courage, honor, and integrity worthy of our cheers.
A small-town boy who grew up on a farm,
Milking cows, feeding chickens, learning to fish, and use a firearm.

Going to church, reading the Bible, and being taught how to pray,
Would instill the morals and values he lives by today.
His college days would allow him to meet
His lifelong partner who would make his life complete.

His demeanor is of a quiet and humble man,
Who is always willing to help and serve where he can.
The military would be his chosen profession
Where his love for soldiers and country would reflect much exceptionalism.

Being a dad and granddad clearly has brought much elation,
Guiding and encouraging his family to stand on a firm foundation.
Swiftly seventy sensational years have flown by,
But he preserves to live productively and continues to aim high.

A Congregational Farewell

(Dedicated to Chaplain Williams)

Time has now come to bid a congregational farewell
To our illustrious pastor that has served us exceptionally well.
His tenure here, at Main Post Chapel, has passed much too fast,
And now, with heavy hearts, we feel sullen and downcast.

His fiery sermons kept our hearts alert and aware,
Preaching God's Word with much passion and flair.
With his heartfelt messages, many lives have been changed,
New hearts awakened and now rearranged.

Now embarking upon retirement,
Many opportunities will unfold with anticipation and excitement.
After twenty-nine years, he faithfully served and answered God's call,
Ministering to many soldiers and civilians befriending all.

Our illustrious chaplain ran his race with a fervent pace,
Spreading the gospel, allowing a multitude to understand the gift of grace.

Sisters in Christ

(Dedicated to Bev, Anita, Marie, Ginny, Cheri, and Ann Marie)

My sisters in Christ are those precious friends I have been blessed to know,
The special ones that have made a difference and helped me to grow.
Those are the sisters I have learned from and can depend,
Who show up in time of trouble with a helping hand to lend.

These angels, as I believe them to be,
All assigned to mentor, encourage, and pray for me.
These special sisters have stood by patiently,
And all have been blessings over thirty years faithfully.

During some of my happiest and darkest days,
These sisters never stopped cheering me on and are worthy of my heartfelt praise.
Although never having a biological sister to grow up with and know,
My sisters in Christ were designated to fill that void with a love that constantly flows.

Those are the sisters I have learned from and can depend,
Who show up in time of trouble with a helping hand to lend.
My sisters in Christ—jewels that I will forever treasure—
Priceless friends that are rare and beyond measure.

About the Author

Patti A. Tucker was born to a loving family and was raised in a small town in Southern West Virginia. She has been an office worker, teacher, full-time mother, and a military wife for nearly thirty-five years. Patti and her husband of fifty-one years have two children. Both have served our nation: a son as a US Marine combat veteran and a daughter who teaches America's youth. They have three grandchildren, the inspiration for her creativity.

Patti's strong trust in God and her undeniable belief in family values guide her steps and her Poetic Praises.

CPSIA information can be obtained
at www.ICGtesting.com
Printed in the USA
LVHW081648260721
693699LV00013B/477